Proclaim It From The Mountains

Aspen Physis

BookLeaf
Publishing

India | USA | UK

Presentation by *BookLeaf Publishing*

Web: www.bookleafpub.com

E-mail: info@bookleafpub.com

ISBN: 978-93-5744-319-7

First edition 2022

DEDICATION

To Vita and my Bestest Friend,

Who I wouldn't have tried without.

PREFACE

Memento Mori
C'est la vie,
A balanced life,
Will be the death of me.

This collection is the ups and downs, mountains and valleys, odds and ends, and everything in-between of my heart and soul, as I try to figure out the biggest mystery known to man: life itself.

I - Welcome

Welcome to a land,
Where everyone is starving,
Where a dry river bed,
Flows with tears of the crying.

Everyone has food to share,
But one can't share with oneself,
And no one will share with one,
And one shares with no one.

Welcome to our land,
She sings the dirge with her band.
She smiles to say hello to the pain,
And old friend come 'round again.

This land is not from across the sea,
This land is you and me, you see.

II - To Love?

I decided once that the answer to the question
was no.
Don't love, don't feel.
But I couldn't kill the plants my heart would
sow.
I tried, I keeled.

I let another take me in,
And felt the searing pain,
I went to convince my heart again,
But couldn't convince my brain.

Why do I feel these feelings?
Why do I laugh and cry?
I'd be a psychopath if I didn't,
But since I do they all ask why.

There's no escape from the questions,
No way to not feel,
I want to curl up and die in the hole in my heart!

But this can't be the last part,
There has to be more, it has to get better,
Look at that, I hoped for a couple of letters.
I don't want to wallow inside me,
But my misery wants to define me.

III - Constant Companions

So plagued by the voices,
The friends inside my head,
Governing my choices,
Wishing I was dead.

They whisper "Sweet nothing,
I'm everything to you."
A dirge they faithful sing,
To me, their one and true.

IV - The Paper Kingdom

Their faces stare at me,
All adorned with jewels,
The clown wants to be free,
The one gets to rule.

The king rides his bicycle,
The slave is in the garden,
The giver of all loses this cycle,
The beggar is rewarded for sin.

Two lovers sit,
In some club rarely seen,
The young man is fit,
The lady is his queen.

V - Emotion Dump

Nicotine, caffeine, methamphetamine,
Anything to help me, feel free,
Escape myself, my hell, my wall I've built inside
myself,
This shell, I'd sell every single possession,
I've ever had and everything I ever will,
If I could just escape, recalibrate,
Maybe delete all my mistakes, my life,
This strife, I wanna fight myself,
Wanna kill with skill my sunken soul,
Dig deep and bury in a hole,
Filled with coal, strike a match and burn,
Stand firm as I watch my stern face,
Melt in place while I try to save face by telling,
Everyone I've ever known that I'm ok.

VI - I'm Sorry

Please excuse me while I cry,
While I pour blood from my eyes,
I'll hide it away later, just don't be surprised,
I wouldn't want to startle you by exposing my
lies,
I'm sorry for the mess, it's just the stress,
Watch your step if you come in, I'm trying my
best,
I have no excuse for my life, I think I'm better
off dead,
But I can't even do that, 'cause I'm laying in bed.
Sorry to let that all slip, I'll tighten my lips,
I don't mean to be a burden on your fragile bliss,
Let me just tuck that away, for a far away day,
When I'm all alone, as I am most days.

VII - Silence

All these words that I write and no one to read
them,
All these thoughts that I think but I don't dare
breathe them.
The darkness within shuns the light,
Hide in the basement the fight.
All these words I say to be ignored,
All these demons I have that are abhorred.
As silence screams the plight of the mime,
So every falling second of my time.

VIII - Looking Glass

"No friend of time!"
"No friend of time!"
The doormouse screams at a quarter to nine.
At quarter to ten he'll say it again,
Now the pattern you know,
For the pattern I've shown.

"Time has no meaning!"
Says the hatter at one,
Go back and he'll scream it at the height of the
sun.
Now at three, then at four, and just a bit more,
The Cheshire cat says that time has got fat.

Fat on the friends that time has not,
And fat on the value that time had got,
And fat on one more thing, his selfish pride,
And now I'm out of time to make this line fit.

IX - How Many?

How many words did you write?
How many songs did you sing?
I could count them all, repeat them all, sing them
all.
If I could bring them back to you, would you
change at all?

Those words like 'always,'
Those words like 'forever,'
Those words are funny things you see, they're
much like 'need,'
And now I see that you don't need me, 'always,'
or 'forever,' or ever at all.

How many tears will I cry?
How many times will I die,
Inside my head, for you, or over you, or in spite
of you?
What if I told you I'd die for you?
Maybe you forgot I did?

Did you love me to leave me?
Did you bend me to break me?

Did I waste all my time, my sleepless nights, all
my fights?
That time I gave to you my dear, that time I can't
get back in life.

How many times will I sit on this floor?
How many times will I stare at this ceiling?
Once I sat, I stared for you; I reached 2000 miles
for you.
I reached and almost felt your hand.
Now I see you drawing it back.
Away from me.
Forever?

X - Scars

I hide my scars but I want them to show,
To show the deep gifts my dear pain left,
To show the neat marks I made under the fog,
The thick fog I made inside my own head.

I still remember the sight of my blood,
Dark red for some reason I can't name,
I wished it to be black, as black as the night,
With the fog that covered the stars in the sky.

In that black night, no sign of clear light,
I found a catharsis, the release that could have killed me.
I still question why, why didn't I die?
God knows I tried.

And maybe that's why,
Maybe that's why I found the stars in the sky,
So I could show them to someone,
Someone like me who hides their scars.

XI - Control

I'm the master puppeteer,
Controlling through my veil of tears,
This entire puppet show,
Of which I'm the lead role.

I'm the prison Warden,
Locking away behind a grin,
All of my emotional sprees,
But I'm not the only one holding keys.

I'm the dealer in this game,
Slinging cards is my middle name,
Looks like I lost to the house,
Because I also have to play the rounds.

I'm this corporation's CEO,
All my wealth will surely grow,
But the thing that fuels my rage,
Is that I get paid minimum wage.

XII - Rabbit Hole

Great Cthulhu whispers "L'appel du vide,"
Soon his call your mind shall heed.
Down rabbit's hole you shall go,
To meet the one who's white as snow.

Perhaps you travel to hobbit's shire,
Or to call King Arthur "Sire,"
One may run to Buttercup's call,
Another to the Elder Wand perhaps will fall.

These inky seas you must explore,
And with cap'n Nemo build rapport.
Whether down that great Icelandic hole,
Or working in 12 mining coal,
This yellow road you shall take,
And another mental world create.

XIII - Notification

I check my phone to get disappointment,
At this point it's just an annoyance.
It's just a screen without your excitement,
It was a box for you to hide in.
Now that you're gone it's nothing special,
It's just so inconsequential.
I still check it for your notification,
But I just start to feel the deflation.

XIV - Failure

I keep failing at everything,
Awake and in my dreams,
I guess failure's just my thing,
Tonight I'm even failing to make myself bleed.

The pain, the sting,
But with no red reward,
No life for me to bring,
No soul to look toward.

Maybe there's nothing left,
I drained myself dry,
Paint myself blessed,
Without it I should die.

Maybe I'm a demon,
They've lived in me so long,
Engulfed by their sin,
I looked into the black dawn.

No blood will come,
My skin I destroy,
No longer is the sun,
My form just a toy.

XV - Cuddling

You're here, in my arms,
You're comforting my every fear,
You're protecting me from every harm,
You're really here.

No distance between us,
Into you I stare,
In you I trust,
You are air.

XVI - Out The Window

The butterfly flies high in the sky,
While the fox frolicks in white socks.
The breeze blows trees with ease,
While the sun shines soft on top.

XVII - Befuddled

I don't know why,
Now I can't rhyme,
I tried to sing,
It came out off key,
I played some wrong notes,
And got a lump in my throat,
I can't play a song,
And I wrote my words wrong.

XVIII - Growth

You worry for me as a frail flower,
Yet failingly paint yourself a strong tower,
Your foundation's cracks may yet be patched,
By a vine with a flower to match.

IXX - Hallelujah

I put on a suit to cover my fears,
And a smile to cover my tears.
Sit in church on Sunday,
Try not to show the fray.
Wear my Sunday best,
To cover my Saturday worst.

XX - Macabre

'Tis midnight on All Hallows Eve,
The wind rushes through boney trees,
The rites are nigh, clouds fill the sky,
Beware, lest all shall die.

'Tis midnight on All Hallows Eve,
The witch draws dagger from her sleeve,
Blood falls red, into cup of the dead,
The ancient words must now be read.

'Tis midnight on All Hallows Eve,
The ritual is read from creed,
The secret words which no man knows,
Are screamed into the wind that blows.

'Tis the wee morn of All Hallows Day,
The witch now has gone away,
The ritual has been proclaimed,
The Evil one more year sustained.

XXI - Farewell

I don't care that this doesn't rhyme,
I don't care about the length of lines.
I don't care the stanzas are different shapes,
I don't care I didn't contemplate,
How to make it fit a mold,
How to get it carved in gold.
This is my pure passion in words,
This is my anger, my sadness, my emotion in
ink.
This is me on a clean white sheet,
Smudged with all these black streaks.

www.ingramcontent.com/pod-product-compliance
Lightning Source LLC
LaVergne TN
LVHW050504210726
843509LV00015BA/2984